"*Understanding Yourself* departs from the jargon of many contemporary psychology books. The handy format and readable prose makes this book an ideal tool for readers who want to understand and change the behaviors that lie at the root of their own unhappiness. With refreshingly simple language and everyday examples, Dr. Boriosi offers real solutions to real life problems."

— **Cheryl Kashuba**

D1548564

Understanding Yourself

It's So Darn Easy

Understanding Yourself

It's So Darn Easy

Guido D. Boriosi, M.D.

Rutledge Books Danbury, CT

The opinions expressed in this publication reflect those of the author. However, the author makes no warranty regarding the contents of the publication. The protocols described herein are general and may not apply to a specific patient.

ALL RIGHTS RESERVED
Rutledge Books, Inc.
107 Mill Plain Road, Danbury, CT, 06811
1-800-278-8533

Manufactured in the United States of America

Cataloging in Publication Data
Understanding Yourself. It's So Darn Easy
    Guido D. Boriosi, M.D.
    ISBN: 1-58244-208-8

    1. Psychology. 2. Human Behavior. 3. Anxieties. 4. Perception of self and reality.

Library of Congress Control Number: 2001098663

This book is dedicated to

My Wife, Catherine

and to

The memory of my parents,

Pacifico and Gina Boriosi

·The Chapters·

ACKNOWLEDGMENTS

Dr. Boriosi gratefully acknowledges the following people for their assistance with the preparation of the manuscript of his book:

Diane Grande

Nancy Reddington Parlo

Laurie Rosin

Cheryl A. Kashuba

and a special "Thanks, TJ" to Toni Jones

How To Read This Book

It is my hope that you will see this book as a simple model for understanding human behavior. Take the sections that make sense and accept them as your own. The parts that are not accepted are to be forgotten. Used with your own information from other sources, this book gives you a model and a concept for understanding human feelings and behavior.

If someone takes swatches of cloth from many old clothes and sews them together to make a new suit, we see there is no new cloth but the suit is an original.

The material in this book has little that is new or original. It consists of information received through experiences in my life from childhood to the present. It comes from contacts with people I've known-parents, clients, friends, and acquaintances-books I've read, lectures I've listened to, personal experiences, and from the masters in the field of psychology. The greatest contributors were my parents. Neither finished their elementary education, but both were wise beyond what any book could teach.

Chapter 1

Plain Talk Psychotherapy

K*I*S*S
We all have to learn to keep it sensibly simple.

Understanding human behavior, learning to live comfortably, and deriving as much pleasure from life as possible are so simple that they are missed by the majority of people. It is my purpose to eliminate the myth of complicated human behavior and replace it with the simplicity and logical understanding that it deserves. The system I use is called:

K*I*S*S
Keep It Sensibly Simple

You must accept two basic premises to follow
this simple concept:
First: I am a human being and I am not God
Second: All other beings I encounter in my life are also
human beings and not God

First Premise: I am a human being and I am not God.

This statement sounds simple, and most people claim to understand it. If you watch most people behave in an interpersonal relationship, you will see that they do not live as if they have accepted this premise. It often becomes difficult for one person in a relationship to accept the errors of the other person. It is only human to ask a person to change some things about themselves. But sometimes they can't or won't change. Then, you have to accept the fact that no change will occur. You can't force another person to submit to your will. Refusing to accept the fact that no change will be made usually heads the relationship for trouble.

There will be many times when things do not go your way. You are human and not God, and because of this you will make errors in your life. Consider this situation. You are a star football player. In a crucial game you fumble the ball on the goal line, and the game is lost. When you review the videotapes, you see that you did indeed fumble the ball. It will be your job to review the tape, learn why you made the fumble, and try not to let it happen again. When you have accepted the fumble, destroy the tape and forgive yourself. Your role as a human is to try not to make errors. However, when you do, there are some things you can do to make the error easier on yourself. First, take time to see the error. Try to understand why it occurred. Learn to avoid making similar errors again. Once you have examined the mistake and learned from it, drop the situation. Know that you have done all you can, and forgive yourself for not being perfect. The nice feature about being human is that errors are permissible.

Your commitment to you, your loved ones, and your God is to give your best effort in anything you do. With this, you have fulfilled your obligation, and the balance rests in a Power greater than yourself.

 Second Premise: All other beings I encounter in my life are also human and not God.

Other people are human, and they, too, will be imperfect. They may be unable or unwilling to change themselves to suit your needs. As you are entitled to be you, they are entitled to be themselves. If we understand this, we can begin to understand one of the major conflicts between human beings: the inability to be happy with another when they are not completely what we want them to be.

There will be times during your life when you will be unacceptable to others because of your humanness and the errors you make. Likewise, you may be not accepted because others are human beings and unable to accept you as you are.

I do not preach religion, but people of the Christian faith may better understand the example of Jesus Christ. Christians accept Jesus Christ as God, perfect. Jesus chose to come and live on earth as man. When He did, there were enough people who disliked this perfect Jesus that He was crucified. How, then, can we expect everyone to like us?

There is only room for One at the top, and the position is taken. The rest of us remain human.

I hope to easily explain how uncomplicated life can be if we simply follow the right road, the road traveled by humans. The road will not always be paved. The road will not always be straight, and heaven knows there will be an abundance of detours. But let me assure you, the journey can be exciting and enjoyable every inch of the way if we let it. Let me share with you some of my thoughts and feelings . . .

·Chapter 2·

The Role of Psychotherapy

You have to choose the therapy that is right for you.

There are a number of schools of psychotherapy-Freudian, Jungian, Rogerian, and others. Many people ask me which school of psychotherapy is right for them. First, no one approach is the right approach. One of the roles of psychotherapy is to develop a better understanding of human behavior. There are many ways to achieve this. A person should pick the type of therapy and therapist that will make them feel the most comfortable.

Second, some therapies are faster than others and more easily understood. Although all therapies should accomplish the same end result, assuming direction is followed, some therapy will get a person to their destination of understanding human behavior faster than others. If you are traveling in Pennsylvania from Scranton to Philadelphia, and you ask for directions, three different people may suggest three different routes. If you are a competent driver, all routes will get you to Philadelphia. Some will just get you there faster. So, too, with various therapies.

Third, you have to get into it to improve the odds. Does this mean that if you go into therapy, you will come out getting everything you want in life-a loving partner, a great job, perfect children? Not necessarily. What you will do is increase the odds of getting as much happiness out of life as you possibly can. This is similar to teaching someone to play cards. Teaching someone to play cards does not guarantee them a win. It does improve the odds so they have the best possible chance to win. So it is with psychotherapy. If people understand human behavior, it does not guarantee them a perfect life with absolute happiness. What it does guarantee is they will have better odds of having happiness in their lives. The actual end result, however, is often out of their control.

Fourth, enjoy the process and free yourself from the end result. Like playing a game of cards, life is easy to enjoy when you are winning. Unfortunately, you cannot always win or get everything you want. Every now and again you will lose the card game, but this does not mean you will have to stop playing the game. So it is with life.

If you take responsibility for your life and give every effort your best shot, you can learn to accept the outcome. Understand that life is a process and try to focus away from end results such as winning or losing. Realize those end results often depend on circumstances and variables beyond your control, such as a degree of intelligence or talent that you receive from God at birth. Psychotherapy can enable individuals to change their focus from the outcome to the process. The joy must come from knowing you did the best you could with what was available to you.

Accept yourself and do not focus on the tyranny of an "end oriented" life. Remember the slogan: "Be all that you can be." This does not mean:
Be all that your parents want you to be, or
Be all that your friends want you to be, or not even to
Be all that you want to be.
Understand that your goal is to do what you are able to do. Do not concentrate on situations in life that are out of reach. Know your abilities and follow the motto:
BE ALL THAT YOU CAN BE!

·Chapter 3·

The Myth of Analytical Psychotherapy

Psychotherapy does not have to mean years
on the couch, drudging up your childhood.

Many people may well be helped by analytical psychotherapy; however, it appears to be very impractical for most.

Analytical therapy starts from the womb or before. You work through your problems. Analytical therapy isn't very logical as a therapeutic tool. It asks you to rehash the bad past again today, tomorrow, and forever. If you have had a bad experience in the past, it may be proper to mentally review it once or maybe twice. You can use tools such as the ones you will learn from this book to try to understand what and how the situation happened. After you do that, put it to rest and get on with your life. The bad experience was bad in the past, and you cannot make it better. Reliving it again today should cause discomfort today, and if we discuss it again next week, it should cause discomfort next week. If we discuss it one year from now, it should also cause discomfort. Analytical therapy seems to be the approach that asks clients to continue to relive the bad experience that keeps them uncomfortable and in need of therapy. Their therapy, in turn, keeps them uncomfortable because it continues to rehash the bad experience. It is difficult to see how the circle will ever end.

An *action-now oriented therapy* places the emphasis on what you can do to improve your situation or the situation of your loved ones. Past experiences should be viewed as learning experiences. If it was pleasant, try to repeat it. If it was unpleasant, try to avoid it.

If you drive across town and your tire goes flat, spend very little time trying to find out why the tire went flat. Rather, spend your energy fixing the tire and getting on your way.

Chapter 4

Inadequacy

*You can understand this powerful
feeling and how to manage it.*

Every human being has feelings of inadequacy. At birth,
infants do not feel inadequate but in reality, these
infants are totally inadequate. They depend on others for
the food, clothing, shelter, love and affection they need for
survival. Their very lives are threatened if they do not have
someone to take care of them.

Depending on circumstances, all human beings are sus-
ceptible to feeling inadequate and vulnerable. The initial
emotional imprint of being dependent on others never really leaves us. Instead, these feelings of inadequacy become
lodged in our unconscious mind, ready to surface when the
right buttons are pushed in emotional situations.
Understand that the unconscious mind does not respond to
the concept of time or age and it does not use reason, so it is
not logical in nature. Given these conditions of the unconscious mind, the feeling of having our lives threatened that

we had as infants is the same feeling that will surface in adulthood when we feel vulnerable. This feeling will be intense and we will feel out of control. Because of this feeling, we go through life looking for the outside environment to protect us. We need positive feedback to go forward in life and not feel threatened.

In early growth and development children need to know and learn that they belong, that they are loved and cared for by their parents. If children build confidence in themselves, "shields" build up around the feelings of inadequacy. As they grow older, their personalities will be dictated by how thick these "shields" have become. Such children grow to be confident individuals.

However, some children are raised by parents who are feeling inadequate themselves. Such parents are unable to provide love and nurturing and thus prevent their children from gaining confidence. Children raised in this manner will grow to have feelings of inadequacy that are easily exposed. Inadequately-nurtured children will have fewer layers of confidence, or fewer "shields," to protect them. It is an unfortunate legacy of being poorly parented.

The need for children to have positive feedback from parents is tremendous. As adults, we seek other sources to continue this positive feedback. Sometimes we compromise our own needs, feelings, and actions to get the approval from significant others. This need is not Aristotelian-like logic, nor is it factual. This may help to explain the intense emotion and irrational (not logical) behavior expressed by people who feel rejected by their significant others.

If you are an adult human being, not psychotic and not severely retarded, you will find that your ability to function in life is not necessarily dependent on other people. Dependency can be *wanted* but is not usually *essential*. If we have stored all of the positive feedback from our environment, we can seek positive feedback from others but know that this feedback is not essential. We should be able to draw from our confidence or inner "shields" knowing that we are, in fact, an adequate person. Initially, this concept is more easily understood than felt.

An inadequate individual is like a cake that feels the icing is necessary to make the cake desirable. A person who has confidence would feel the cake was good whether or not it had icing. However, if it did have icing, it would be an even better cake.

·Chapter 5·

Conscious vs. Unconscious

Make conscious decisions

Logical mind vs. Emotional mind

Making sense vs. No reasoning

The human mind is composed of the *Conscious*, which is rational, and the *Unconscious*, which is emotional. Human behavior is motivated by both the conscious and unconscious mind. Both contribute to the reasons for our actions.

The conscious mind is rational. It is the mind we think with, the one we use when listening or conversing. It is the mind that uses Aristotelian-like logic. When it functions properly, the conscious mind is logical.

The unconscious mind is emotional and uses a primitive logic called paleologic. It works on the Pleasure Principle, showing no reasoning for its actions. It understands like or dislike, yes or no, on or off. The unconscious mind does not work within the concept of time. Therefore, some impressions that are emotional in nature and implanted in our mind at an early age can be aroused many years later.

For example, as children, we may have learned that snakes may be life threatening, so we grow to be afraid of snakes. In adult life, if we see a harmless garden snake, our conscious or logical mind will tell us that this snake is not a threat to our life. Our unconscious or emotional mind, however, will still respond as it did when we were children. We will fear death from the snake, although we may try to rationalize our fear by saying it is just a matter of not liking the snake.

Often it is more than one force that motivates a human being. Think of a tug of war game. If you watch the center of the rope in a game of tug of war, it will move in the direction of the greater force, as if that were the only force acting on the rope. When you see all of the players, you become aware there were also many forces pulling in the opposite direction. Or think of a mathematical vector where a variety of forces are pulling in many directions. It sometimes appears the most obvious force is the reason for a specific result. Upon closer inspection, it is revealed that the multitude of forces is the actual cause of the result.

These examples illustrate the difference between what appears to be real and what actually is real. Like the mathematical vector or the tug of war rope, what motivates a person often turns out not to be a simple matter.

When you find yourself in a difficult situation, the advice of family may have a very logical basis. The logic of your own conscious mind can have the same logical components as the advice that the family gave, but the unconscious, emotional component will be different. And that will be strictly yours. This explains why family and friends are unable to understand your actions or emotions in some situations. They are unable to understand your personal emotional feelings.

Consider this example. It may be easy for parents to tell their daughter to leave a difficult relationship. Leaving would be the logical thing to do. The daughter may have difficulty leaving this relationship if, in fact, the relationship has tremendous emotional fulfillment for her such as companionship or children. The parents, using the logic of the conscious mind, see their daughter is unhappy in the relationship. They do not see the daughter's concerns for any positive emotions returned by the relationship. (Spouse, social companion, father present at home for the children, etc.)

If we visualize this situation as on a scale, we will have:

Left side: the parents use logic and see no positive input from the relationship and

Right side: the daughter can see some negatives in the relationship. This is countered by some positives in the emotional drive such as having a social companion, possible financial security, or wanting children raised in a two-parent household.

It is important to remember that we use both the conscious (logical) and unconscious (emotional) minds when making decisions.

Understanding this, we can see that someone who is using good logic may act in a manner different from what we expect. They may not be "crazy" or "stupid" but may have different emotional input into the situation resulting in an entirely different consequence.

Chapter 6

Defense Mechanisms

*Sublimation-Projection-Denial-Displacement
Our mental health depends on using
defense mechanisms.*

Human beings use a wide variety of defense mechanisms to handle the anxiety that results from feeling inadequate. Defense mechanisms are unconscious in nature. We use defense mechanisms to manage stress so it will not overwhelm us. Some of these mechanisms are healthy, and some are pathological. You should be aware that we use both healthy and pathological defense mechanisms.

When you are psychologically healthy, you most often use good defense mechanisms and less often use pathological defense mechanisms. When you are ill, you most often use pathological defense mechanisms and less often use healthy defense mechanisms.

The following are a few important examples of some defense mechanisms. Understanding these defense mechanisms will help you understand yourself and the people around you.

Sublimation

One of the best defense mechanisms is *sublimation*. Some people have negative inner drives-such as anger, aggression, or hostility-that can cause problems. Sublimation involves learning to convert the anger into a positive act that is socially acceptable. People who use sublimation take that which is bad and turn it into good.

Contact sports such as football and boxing are examples of sublimation of aggression. People make very lucrative livings as professional athletes. Once on the field or in the ring, they are able to rid themselves of their aggression in a way that is socially acceptable.

Projection

Another defense mechanism we use is *projection*. The term *projection* is very descriptive. You have an inner feeling that makes you unhappy, so you project it and pretend it is coming from another source. If you have a psychiatric illness and are paranoid, projection is the predominant defense mechanism. Healthy people who are not paranoid will use this defense mechanism less frequently.

Consider this simple example. If I wear a tie that I am not comfortable with and I see someone staring at the tie, I say to myself, "She is staring at my tie because she thinks it is not nice." I am the one who is uncomfortable with the tie, but I am projecting the dislike onto someone else.

How many times have you thought, "I do not think that person likes me"? You do not really know if that person does or does not like you, but you project an unknown fact of dislike onto them. It is your feeling of insecurity that makes you feel you are not likable.

Denial

Another common defense mechanism is *denial*. There are two terms that sound alike yet are very much different: *denying* and *denial*.

Denying is a *conscious* phenomenon. When we deny, we use the logical mind. When we do something we are aware is wrong or not acceptable, we may consciously deny having done or said it. Claiming "I did not do that" and knowing that you did is denying.

The second term, *denial*, is a defense mechanism. The denial defense mechanism looks very much the same as denying, but it is done automatically on an *unconscious* basis. If you say or do something that does not fit your personality or that makes you very uncomfortable, you block it out of your conscious mind and are convinced you did not say or do this thing.

For example, you are in a conversation with a group of friends, and you state something incorrectly. Your friends correct you, and you say, "No, I did not say that." You really believe you have not made the statement. You have no recall of it. Yet, several other people, who heard you, could say, "Yes, you did say it that way." This is a classic example of denial.

If someone were to challenge you in terms of your conscious awareness of having said something improperly, they would find you truly do not believe you have said it improperly. Yet, the fact that other people heard you means that indeed you said it as they heard it. Blocking something out of the conscious mind is *denial*. If you know you made an error but are not about to admit it, that is *denying*. An adult who constantly uses denial may be also known as a pathological liar.

Denial is the predominant defense mechanism in children. Children use denial as a way of defending themselves from anxiety. For example, you bake cookies and warn your son not to touch them. You leave the room, and when you return, the child's hand is in the cookie jar. When you ask what the child is doing, he responds "Nothing." When you say, "Don't lie to me. You have your hand in the cookie jar," he replies "No, I don't." You get angry and reprimand the child for lying to you. What you do not understand is that the child was so afraid of what would happen that he actually believed his hand was not in the cookie jar. The child believes he is not taking the cookie because believing he is taking it is traumatic. When the child said he was not taking the cookie, the denial was his defense mechanism. To an adult, such actions would be considered lying.

Children who have had a difficult upbringing and/or have experienced trauma in their lives will rely on denial for survival. The practice of denial will stay with them through most of their early growth and development. It becomes a predominant defense mechanism for them.

Let me share a personal experience. I adopted my daughter when she was six years of age. She is a wonderful girl, but denial is part of her defense mechanism. She was placed in an orphanage at age five and bounced around to several foster homes. Tammy came to us as a foster child. I remember playing with her after work one day. She wrapped her arms around me and said, "Daddy!" Denial. She denied her own mother and father for their not being with her and was willing to believe and accept me as her father. If traumatic experiences are part of a child's early life, denial may become one of her main defenses in adult life.

Human behavior is not cut and dry. Well-adjusted human beings use denial less frequently. As we grow older, we increase the use of "good" defenses such as sublimation.

Displacement

Finally, a fourth defense mechanism you should be

aware of is displacement. Adults use displacement a great deal. When we vent our feelings of anxiety or trauma on a person or object other than that for which it was intended, we use displacement.

For example, if your spouse is having an affair, you really should be angry with your spouse. But many people direct their anger to the person with whom the spouse is having the affair. Doing so is an example of displacement. This person loves his spouse and is afraid of losing her. He feels he cannot afford more negative feeling toward his spouse. What he does is vent all of his anger and frustration on the third party, when in fact, the proper feeling of anger should be toward the spouse.

As human beings, we are intelligent, aware of the future, and aware of our mortality and death, but the mortal concept of death is unknown to us. Human beings are never comfortable with unknowns, and this causes us a great deal of concern and difficulty. How many of us walk around thinking about death and dying? Very, very few, and very rarely. Much of the anger and frustration we experience when things are not going our way is displaced *from* thoughts of death *to* the particular situation we have at hand.

When first starting my practice, I did consultations in the intensive care unit of a local hospital. Many patients I saw were prominent business people or professionals. I got the feeling that prior to their very serious medical illnesses, the worse possible stress they had was closing a particular business deal or worrying about their family. Now that their lives were threatened, they realized that the weight of emotion they had given to those business deals was no longer important. The financial worry of providing for a family was no longer a priority. The only matter of importance was their lives. At that point in my career, I decided I would try to make people aware that the thought of death is the ultimate threat. The real intensity of those business deals lies not in the situation, but in the defense mechanism of displacement.

Chapter 7

Ambivalence

---

*Feeling both negative and positive
emotions at the same time.*

*A*mbivalence is a lot like moving in opposite directions. It is north and south, plus and minus, love and hate. It is the presence of both negative and positive emotions at the same time.

If we truly care for someone and love them deeply, the positives will always outweigh the negatives. The negatives will be almost unnoticeable. You love your mother. She is the most wonderful person in the world. You can be assured that if she is human there were times you felt some hatred rise against her. Because you love her so much, that minute feeling of hatred gets lost.

Likewise, on the negative side, if you have strong feelings of discomfort or hatred for someone, you may not be aware of any of the positive feelings you might have. If you have a neighbor whom you strongly dislike and you can find no positive qualities about him, the negative feeling will outweigh any positive feeling you may have for him. In either case, strong positive or strong negative feelings provide us with very few difficulties. The emotional mind has no logic, so we either like something or we do not like it. It is when our feelings of love and hate become almost equal that we have difficulties that may cause severe anxiety or influence our decision-making. These are difficult ambivalent states. Our emotions fluctuate and can cause confusion and anxiety.

In most situations where there is emotional involvement, there is a degree of ambivalence. If you are having marital difficulties, you may find yourself in a truly ambivalent state. You have the strong positive feeling of love while at the same time you have strong negative feelings of hate for your spouse. Your emotions are torn in two directions.

Ambivalent feelings are characteristic of human beings and not necessarily indicative of mental illness.

Chapter 8

Anxiety of Anticipation

When you anticipate something, you
feel anxiety about it.
You can understand better how to manage
that anticipation.

It is pretty much universal that the anxiety of anticipation always exceeds the anxiety of an event or action. The degree of anxiety is not based on what will actually happen. Rather, the degree of anxiety lies in anticipation.

Anticipation is based on the thoughts surrounding a situation that is not real, has not yet arisen, or has not yet happened. These thoughts can be classified as *fantasies*. You should understand that human beings are incapable of fantasizing intermediately. We always fantasize to the maximum, whether it is *maximum positive* or *maximum negative*. Rarely will what you anticipate be an accurate reflection of what the outcome will be. The outcome usually will be less than the maximum worst or maximum best, such as: You may not do as poorly as you expected to on a test, or you may not have as enjoyable a time as imagined on your vacation.

Consider this example. During a routine examination, your doctor finds a lump and schedules tests. Your test results are good, but more testing will be required. Immediately you have negative thoughts of cancer, treatments, decisions about your personal life, and thoughts of your impending death. You are fantasizing to the *maximum negative*.

You don't first anticipate that the lump is just a lump with no other effects or treatment required, nor do you fantasize that it is a benign cyst. Such fantasies would be the *intermediate negative*. Anticipating-or fantasizing about-the outcome of a situation will always bring anxiety.

Understanding this concept should help you to see a doctor as soon as possible if you suspect something is wrong. Whatever the doctor finds will not cause as much anxiety as fantasizing about the problem. Address a difficult situation quickly rather than waiting and anticipating the outcome.

Anxiety is also associated with anticipating the *maximum positive*. If you find a lottery ticket lying on the street, your mind will immediately focus on the fantasy of being a winner. Never will you think of being a $5 winner. Instead, you will picture yourselves on the cruise ship counting your millions. You will fantasize to the *maximum positive*.

All human beings have the anxiety of anticipation, and it rarely approximates the anxiety of the action.

Chapter 9

Evolution of Emotions

Our emotions are complex,
but we can understand them better.

Human beings are emotional in nature, and some carry their emotions closer to the surface than others. That is what gives us different personalities. You should understand that if you can laugh when you are happy, you should be able to accept that you will cry when you are sad.

At times, we may not know why we have a particular mood because our mood will not be based on anything logical. If you recall, we talked about human beings having two drive mechanisms. One is a conscious logical mind—an Aristotelian-like logical drive mechanism. The other is an unconscious, non-logical, and non-Aristotelian mind that works on the pleasure principle. This non-logical, unconscious mind has no time sequence. It can stimulate an emotional response that was present from a much earlier time in your life.

A child is riding in a car that has a slight fender-bender. The two drivers have "threatening" words with each other with the child witnessing the argument. This child could construe the fender-bender as a threatening phenomena.

Many years later, the child, now grown up, witnesses a fender-bender in front of his house. The two drivers are shouting at each other. The witness's intellectual brain may hardly notice the incident because it does not involve him. Later, he may find that he is having tremendous emotional upheaval, with feelings of discomfort, anxiety, and/or depression, and maybe even loss of sleep. He may not understand, logically, what the reason is for his mood, unless he is able to understand the dynamics that were involved with the accident.

Use your logical mind when trying to understand emotions. Humans have many moods and should try to control their responses to these moods to the best of their ability.

Chapter 10

Human Emotions

Everyone has emotions. Trying to deny them
does no good. They can be helpful allies.

Human beings have a range of emotions from total happiness to total misery. It is not essential for you to live
in a constant state of happiness. Many people get into difficulties because they can't accept the fact that, as human
beings, there will be times when they are unable to control
situations or moods.

Since the era of television and advertising, we are constantly bombarded with the idea that there must be a pill to
take for a constant state of bliss. We can go from pain to
comfort by taking a pill. We can take pills for constipation,
diarrhea, arthritis, depression, and even for sex. The message is that there must be something wrong if we are not in
a constant happy state, and we keep looking for a quick fix.

There are times when it is perfectly normal to be nerv-
ous, depressed, angry, or unhappy. We should be able to

withstand the varieties of emotions that we have. Only if the emotion is not consistent with the situation at hand should we explore remedies.

Chapter 11

Thoughts vs. Actions

It is not how you think or feel, but how you choose to act that is important.

A human mind has free-flowing thoughts and feelings, and it would be a vain attempt to try to control them. If we try to totally control our thoughts, they may become diverted and present themselves in different forms. If you become angry with someone, direct the anger at the person who made you angry. You may try to modify your expression of anger but don't try to *deny* the anger. If you do, you may find yourself later screaming at an innocent bystander.

The only real control you can assert is how you choose to act.

I think about robbing banks, but I am able to control my actions and not act on robbing a bank. Thus I am not a bank robber. Controlling our actions takes time, effort, and discipline but as humans we often act impulsively in a neurotic manner. Neurotic refers to the emotional part of your mind, the part not controlled by logic. Our neurotic thoughts may be helpful, but they may also hold us back. We should attempt to discipline ourselves to act in a non-neurotic fashion and not worry about the associated thoughts and feelings. At times we may have to play the role with our actions. If the role-playing is ego-syntonic, it will be easy to do.

It is not what you think or feel but how you choose to act that is important. Some people cannot enjoy their good behavior because they worry that their thoughts and feelings are inappropriate. Understand that people are recognized for their actions and good behavior. We have no way of knowing about their thoughts and feelings. People we recognize as good people are judged by their actions, what they say and what they do. They are not judged by how they feel, since we are not privileged to that information.

Chapter 12

Choosing Good vs. Bad

Life would be simple if we had only two choices:
good or bad.
But life has gray areas. It is
important to accept your humanness
and make the choice that is best for a given situation.

Life would be so simple if we had only two choices-good or bad. Unfortunately most situations are not that easily solved.

As children, we are taught that if we are good, all good things will happen to us . . . but if we are bad, only bad things will happen. This belief stays with us and, as we grow, we often find ourselves in situations that make us uncomfortable, assuming we are doing something wrong, or bad. Our childhood teachings tell us there must be something available to us that we can do to make everything right, or good. This is simply not true. We often find we do not get to choose right (good) or wrong (bad). Many times our choices will be between bad and worse; good will not be an option to us. It is important to know that when the choices are bad or worse, whichever we pick as the choice we must accept. Although we may not like the choices, we cannot complain about them since the good option was not available to us. The option we choose is as good as it can get.

I am sure everyone has taken a test that has multiple choice answers. After reviewing answers to a particular question, you realize you did not like any of the answers available to you. Maybe you even decided you could devise a better answer, one that would be exactly right. In reality, you are unable to do this. You cannot afford to leave the question unanswered, for fear of failing the test. You have to go back to the answers provided and choose the best answer among those given. After making your choice, you must accept the fact that you chose the best answer available to you.

If we learn to accept our humanness, living with the bad option does not make us feel good, but we will more easily accept the bad choice.

Many times human beings have to accept the gray areas in life because black and white areas are not always available.

Consider these other instances. Your doctor tells you that you need cancer surgery. You are stuck between two choices, (1) bad: surgery, and (2) worse: continued progression of the disease. (There is no good, not needing the surgery is not a choice available to you.) You can choose to go home with the pain and probably get worse, or you can suffer through the surgery with some hope of getting better. Neither option is good, but you must make what you feel will be the better of the two choices.

Here is an example of how the principle of good and bad choices works in our everyday lives. After working all day, you look forward to going home to relax. As you enter the house, your spouse is waiting for you with reservations to a favorite restaurant. You have no good choices in this situation. As tired as you feel, going out to dinner will be a bad choice, but not going will be a worse choice because it will lead to your spouse's anger and disappointment. You will have to make the best choice of the two options given to you: to go out or not to go out. Remember, if you choose to go out to dinner, make the best of your decision and have an enjoyable evening since it was *your* best choice. Doing something that was best for you under the circumstances, and having someone you care for benefit from it, can only be felt as a positive choice.

Chapter 13

Opinion vs. Fact

*Opinions can never be "wrong" because
they express a point of view. Be open
to expressing your opinions and to
learning from other people's opinions.*

The fact is, you could never be wrong about your opinion. Here lies the difference between opinion and fact.

Every human being is entitled to an opinion, and we can never be wrong about our opinion. There will be no arguments if we indicate that our discussion revolves around opinion. Most arguments arise because opinions are presented as facts. A statement of fact requires proof of the fact to satisfy others. An opinion does not require proof. It is important to make clear that you are presenting an opinion rather than a statement of fact.

If it is my opinion that the cherubs on the legs of my desk are gold, it is just that, my opinion and I cannot be wrong about my opinion. If I make a statement of fact that the cherubs on the legs of my desk are gold, then I better have the bill of sale from the store to prove that fact.

Opinions are never wrong since they express a point of view.

Facts are subject to a true-false test because they must be proven.

You should feel free to express your opinion, for in doing so, you encourage other people to do the same. Others may have the knowledge to express new facts. In either case, you invite good conversation and the possibility to learn.

If you understand these statements, you should never be uncomfortable expressing your opinion.

Chapter 14

Success vs. Failure

*If we accept ourselves as human and give
the maximum effort in
everything we do, we will never fail.*

If we accept ourselves as human and attempt to give the maximum effort to succeed in what we do, we will never fail. We fail only when we give less than the maximum effort. We may fail to complete a project, but by giving 100% effort we have not failed in terms of our responsibility as human beings.

When we begin a project, we must put our maximum effort into it. If the project is successful, that success is a bonus. If it does not succeed, we must understand we are human and that some projects will require talents we may not have been given by God. We can put this unsuccessful project right alongside of the others we have accumulated.

The key to success is the **R & A** factor:

Take **R**esponsibility for your life. Give 100% effort and try to accomplish your goals. You will see that the end result is not what determines your successes. Success or failure is determined by the amount of effort you desire to contribute.

Focus on **A**cceptance of your humanness. Understand you are not God. You are imperfect, make mistakes, and sometimes fail at tasks. You must learn to **A**ccept defeat but continue to try new tasks.

At birth, you are given certain talents and abilities, but you are not given the specifics of these talents.

You are a good swimmer and qualify for the swim team at school. You give your every effort to win at a meet but come in last. You did not fail. Losing has nothing to do with you as a person. All it says is that you were not the best swimmer at the competition. You can be disappointed but not defeated. You took **R**esponsibility for yourself and competed in the meet, giving maximum effort to win. Now you must accept the loss. This **A**cceptance will free you to try other challenges in your life and find other talents and abilities you may have. Remember that whatever the outcome of the situation, keep trying.

There is a clear distinction between failing and being unable to complete or understand a situation. Finding you are unable to complete or understand something can be disappointing, but it is not failure. Because we are human, we have encountered these situations before. No doubt we will be faced with them again.

The **R** & **A** Factor:

Responsibility of giving the maximum effort to each day.
Acceptance of knowing you are human.

Chapter 15

Never Take a Hint

Open communication is essential for
healthy human interaction.
Don't take hints.

A hint is part of a statement. It is partial and not accurate. It does not give the full facts, the issue is not clearly stated, and the message can be misconstrued. Hints can be verbal (statements that leave you with the impression that the person didn't say everything they meant to say) or they can be non-verbal. A hint is dependent on your fantasy, not necessarily on what was really meant. You should not want to make decisions based on fantasy when facts are available.

You are walking toward someone and he suddenly turns away. If the person does not want to talk to you, he should clearly explain his action. You may not be happy about it, but you should not let it overwhelm you. However, the individual could have turned away for many other reasons, none of which had anything to do with you.

If someone has something to say to you, he should be willing to say it directly to you. A statement should be directed to the person for whom it is intended. You do not necessarily have to like what is being said, but you should be willing to accept it. Listen to the person's full statement. Taking hints or parts of a statement can only lead to difficulties. A hint will never give a complete statement. It is based on fantasy and not facts, and it can lead to erroneous decisions.

Never take a hint.

Chapter 16

Knowing What To Do

*We often become immobilized because we
do not know what to do. Sometimes
it is enough to know what we are not going to do.*

I would like to point out that many times we become immobilized because we feel we do not know what to do in some situations. At such times, we can have tremendous feelings of inadequacy. We are stymied because our emotions would like us to know what is happening and to know that the result will end properly.

Since we are human beings and cannot foretell the future, it will be difficult to make a decision that will be perfect. Sometimes it is sufficient to know what we are not going to do.

Many years ago I was in graduate school working on my Ph.D. in research and biochemistry. It became obvious to me after one semester that this work was certainly not ego-syntonic for me. It was causing me a great deal of anxiety, although I was capable of doing the work. I can still recall phoning my parents to tell them I was leaving school at the end of that semester. My mother asked, appropriately, "Well, what are you going to do?" I told her I didn't know what I was going to do, but I did know what I was not going to do. I wasn't going to stay in school and prepare for a future that would make me unhappy. She asked, "If you come home and don't like what you're doing here, then what?"

There I sat, not knowing what to do, but very sure that I would not continue in research. I was unable to know at that time what the future would bring, but I was willing to make the move and try to find a position that would be ego-syntonic to me.

In some situations, when we begin to panic about knowing what to do, it might be advisable to stop and think. See if the answer lies in what we should *not* do.

Chapter 17

Telling The Truth: Good Judgment

*Always telling the truth may be as neurotic
as always telling a lie.*

If you were to testify in court, you would be asked to tell the truth, the whole truth, and nothing but the truth. In everyday life, a human being who is *always* telling the truth is as neurotic as someone who is *always* telling lies.

I go to my doctor, who has a collection of ugly ties. He asks me if I like the tie he is wearing, which is one of the worst I have seen on him. My judgment will tell me to lie and say the tie is nice. My goal is not to upset him and not to get him angry. I have nothing to gain by telling him the tie is bad.

Part of a normal mental status is a phenomenon called judgment. Your judgment should dictate what you say and when you say it. Most importantly, judgment dictates whether to tell the truth. Keep in mind, we should have a goal to achieve when we speak or act.

Let your judgment dictate what you say to people.

Here is another example. I am walking down Lackawanna Avenue, and someone who is three times my size tells me to cross the street and walk on the other side. If my goal is to see which of us is stronger, my judgment would advise me to tell him to get lost. I risk getting thrown to the ground and beaten. All I would have proven is that he could hurt me. If my goal was not to get hurt or test my strength and to still get down the street, I would say "Yes, sir" and run across the street.

The truth of the matter is that I had every right to stay on his side of the street. I could have stayed and argued the point with him, but my judgment tells me this person is not going to listen, and I am probably going to get a beating. In this situation, telling the person the truth would be considered neurotic (not logical).

When you say or do anything with another person or persons, you should have a goal in mind-what are you trying to achieve. If what you say or do gives you a chance to attain your goal, your judgment is good. If what you say or do has no opportunity to achieve your goal, and still worse, if it makes achieving your goal less possible, then you are using poor judgment.

Because you are human and not God, there will be many times when your goal cannot be achieved. Doing nothing is your best choice at that time.

Let me share with you a true personal scenario. My parents had sixty-three years of marriage when dad died. Somewhere in their fiftieth year of marriage, while I was visiting, the following took place:

Mom was making soup. She had cooked meals practically every day of her married life. My father, now a retired coal miner, was able to voice his infinite wisdom on all home activities. On this occasion, he told Mom, "I think you should put more salt in the soup." With this, Mom became frustrated and said, "I have made soup for you for fifty years, and now you can do it better?" I pulled Mom aside and said, "Mom, you sure do like to argue." Now she was upset with me. "I like to argue?" she asked. "Didn't you hear your father tell me how to make soup?" I replied, "Yes, I did, but you're the one who must like to argue."

Now, what is this all about? If Mom's goal was to argue, she succeeded, and what she said to my father was in keeping with her goal. However, if her goal was to inform Dad that she knew how to make soup, what she said was a neurotic statement since continuing the conversation only led to an argument. If the goal was to make good soup and not to argue, all she needed to say was, "Okay," and then proceed to make the soup as she had done for fifty years.

Remember:

1. Know *your* goal

2. Make sure what you say or do gives you a chance to achieve *your* goal.

Chapter 18

Decisions

Six steps to easy decision making.

How many times have you dreaded making a decision, fearing you would make the wrong choice? If you want to count yourself among those who can choose and not regret your choice, get into the art of decision making following these six steps:

[Realize there is not a bad decision
     [Recognize the fifty-percenter
          [Not making a decision is a decision
               [Take it a step at a time
                    [Focus away from end results
                        [Acceptance

Step 1) Realize there is no bad decision
Use the Information + Emotion (I + E) Equation

In order to free yourself from the "I should have's" you must recognize from the start there is no such thing as a bad decision—but you may not get the results you want from that decision.

Why?

Think about how you make a decision:

Take into account all the Information available to you. In fact, you might add even more information to what you already have by talking over your decision with friends, reading, or by seeking others who have faced the same dilemma.

Add to the Information your own Emotions. Now you have your unique way of looking at the situation and making a decision. Perhaps because only you know how you really feel, others can empathize or give advice, but never really make the right decision for you. This is because all others may have the same **I** (Information) but the **E** (Emotion) part of the equation is specific to you.

With your own **I + E Equation** *you will make a decision attempting to get the best result.* Because you are human, however, you have limited intelligence and can never foresee the future, nor can you ever know all of the possible facts. Therefore, the end result you get may not always be what you wanted or expected.

THIS DOES NOT MEAN YOU ARE STUPID OR THAT THE DECISION YOU MADE WAS BAD. IT WAS THE BEST DECISION YOU COULD HAVE MADE WITH WHAT WAS AVAILABLE TO YOU AT THAT TIME.

Step 2) Recognize the fifty-percenter

Decision-making can be like coming to a fork in the

road. At a particular point, you must make a left or a right turn. You are unsure which is the correct road. You must choose one of them and turn onto that road, understanding that you have a fifty-fifty chance of making the right or wrong choice. You are not *smart* if you choose the correct road, and you are not *stupid* if you choose the wrong road. You had no way of knowing in advance which road was correct or wrong. It is not fair, having chosen the wrong road, to tell yourself, "I should have known it was the other road." If you had known it was the other road, you would have taken it. Do not look back and get angry for making the wrong choice. In reality, you got the wrong result from making a decision, as a human being, with the knowledge **(I)** and feeling **(E)** you had available at that time.

Step 3) Not making a decision is a decision

There are many times when we feel we cannot make a decision. At the same time, there are many instances when not making a decision is a decision. We know that with the passing of time, decisions that have a time limit to them will have to resolve themselves. There are numerous times when we feel there is no solution to a problem, only to find that with the passing of time, the problem resolves itself. For example, a student in high school is applying to various colleges. He has difficulty making an immediate definite decision about what school to apply to and misses some application deadlines. Now the student cannot apply to several of the schools. By not making the decision to apply before the closing date, the student eliminated those schools.

Step 4) Take it a step at a time

Looking at the overall problem before you make any decision is a wise move. It broadens your scope and gives you a sense of what you must deal with in making your decision. However, if you attempt to have all of the answers to a complex problem at the start, you're setting yourself up for failure and frustration.

Remember to divide your problem into segments, like dividing a pie. Take a piece nearest to you first and deal with it. Take other pieces at other times. You have recently had your annual physical. Your physician calls to tell you about an abnormality in the tests. This is where you handle the first problem first. Accept the situation and get further information regarding the condition. Then go on to the next step. Don't contemplate such things as treatments and surgery before knowing the answers to the initial problem. Only after dealing with the first step should you go on to the next. Things change as time passes. There is no way to know ahead of time what the problem will look like twenty-four hours from now, let alone twenty-four months from now. Keep yourself focused on one issue at a time. Have the confidence in your ability to focus on the next step at the proper time.

Step 5) Focus away from end results

Recognize decision-making is a process, not something strictly geared to end results. Assuming you give the issue your full consideration, and make a decision based on that, you are doing your part. Remember, taking responsibility is crucial to success.

Since the outcome may be beyond your personal control, don't punish yourself by feeling you "made the wrong choice" if you don't get the result you wanted.

You have made the best choice with the Information and Emotions that you had. What really happened is that you got "the wrong result." So, lighten up. You are human. Only God would have made a perfect decision.

Step 6) Acceptance

Finally, pat yourself on the back for having the discipline to learn the art of making a decision and accepting the outcome.

Realize that sometimes a positive outcome is just not in the cards. Some things are beyond your control. To let an outcome adversely affect you for any long period of time is unhealthy.

Although you might not like a particular outcome, learn to live with it. In the long run, you will be glad you did.

Chapter 19

Telling The Question

*If you ask a question when you
want to make a statement,
you are setting up an argument. Always tell
what you want another person to know
instead of asking for their permission to
think or do something.*

I am sure you have heard of making a statement and you
have also heard of asking a question. But do you know
about *telling the question*? We tell the question often, and we
do it mostly in our interpersonal relationships.

When you ask someone a question, it is their prerogative to answer or not to answer your question. If their answer is "yes" and the response is what you wanted, all is well. If their answer is "no," you should abide by it and try to feel good about the negative response. Remember, by asking the question, you are requesting an answer. Do not ask a question if you know that a negative answer will upset you. You are setting up the other person for an argument. In an adult relationship, you need to make a state-ment and not ask permission. Do not give the other person the option of giving an answer you might not want unless you are prepared to handle it. Instead, *tell* the other person what you want them to know. In other words, don't ask a question. *Make a statement.*

A client once told me she and her spouse were going to have an argument when she got home that evening. She explained that whenever she asked her spouse if she could go to New York with her friends, he said no, and an argu-ment would surely follow. When I asked her if she would pass on the trip, as her husband requested, she said she would go anyway. I explained that she was setting up her spouse for the argument. By asking permission to go to New York, she puts herself in a subordinate position, the position of a child to a parent. She gives her spouse the right to say yes or no to the question. If she puts herself in such a position, she should abide by his answer, not quarrel, and make the best of it.

If she could not accept the negative response from her spouse, then she should not ask the question. She should simply tell him she is going to New York. He may get angry and yell, but he can't argue because the decision has been made. Her spouse has the right to object by venting, but there should be no argument because there was no ques-tion. It would be more pleasant if he approved of her going on her trip, but she does not need his approval. She will go regardless.

If you are not comfortable making a statement first, you can ask a reality-oriented question that is not controversial, such as, "How do you feel about my going to New York?" With this, you are not requesting permission but getting the other person's opinion about your activity. You may then use the response as part of the criteria for making your decision. As an equal adult, the decision is yours to make.

It is important that we use commonsense and be direct, whether we are asking a question or making a statement.

Chapter 20

Know Your Boundaries

We all have limitations. It is important to know our own boundaries.

Your most prized possession in this life is YOU. It is your responsibility as an adult to take care of yourself to the best of your ability. Take pride in yourself and your actions.

Many times we get into difficulties when we do not understand where our boundaries begin and end. Naturally, each person, as a human being who is not psychotic or severely retarded, is responsible for himself. It is when we take it upon ourselves to interfere in the lives of others that we find ourselves crossing the boundary line. Since we are human and not God, we cannot be responsible for solving the problems of other human beings. There are three steps to follow before you can cross your boundary line and be involved in the lives of others:

STEP ONE: The other party must ask for your help or be

willing to accept your help. Once they do so,

STEP TWO: You must decide if you want to give your help to them, and

STEP THREE: You must ask yourself if you have the ability to give your help.

If any of these steps is missing, *do not become involved*.

You can think of having boundaries as being similar to someone who owns property. It is important that you care for your property within your own boundaries the best you can. You may have opinions about the adjoining properties, but they are only your opinions and not those of the neighbors. You can only share your thoughts with your neighbors should they ask you for them and should you choose to give these thoughts to them. Frequently, we are not sure where our yard ends, and at times we impose our views across the boundary lines. This can lead to difficulties. We may very well end up taking full responsibility for our neighbor's yard, and we will not have the physical or legal power to do so. This can lead to total frustration. Take full responsibility only for the things you can control.

Stay within your boundaries and take care of your own yard before venturing into unknown territory.

Chapter 21

Selfishness

*Selfishness can serve us well, if we
understand it and use it properly.*

"Don't be selfish." We have heard these words since childhood. In our culture, in the way we are raised, being known as selfish has negative connotations. I would like to propose to you that there are at least two types of selfishness.

The first type of selfishness can be termed *egocentricity*. This is the negative type of selfishness and is probably the one with which we are all familiar. It is characterized by actions or attitudes that are done solely for our own pleasure, with little or no regard for how others are affected. We treat the other party as an object that exists solely for our own use.

Recognize examples of negative selfishness. It can lead to manipulation of others, such as when a man tells a woman he loves her but in reality he only wants to have sex.

This negative selfishness is hurtful and should go against your human feelings.

The second type of selfishness can be termed *selfish positive*, or *self-fulfilling*. We all want to give help when it is needed. However, there are times when we have to take instead of give. We all have to do things to help and please ourselves. *Doing so allows us to become stronger and more complete people and gives us the strength to then continue to help others.* Think of a die hard battery. It constantly gives off charges to help your car run, but be assured: if at times it did not receive a charge, it would surely do as its name suggests, **die hard**.

I constantly remind clients they have to at times think about themselves. These clients usually argue that it is selfish for them to put themselves before others. It is ego-alien (not making sense to you). It is important to have balance in giving and taking in order to have balanced lives. You cannot afford to devote your entire life to everyone else or you will find yourself drained and unable to continue to function. You need to fulfill your own needs or you will deteriorate, be unable to help others, and become a liability to yourself and others.

For example, if I am the only surgeon available on a battlefield and casualties are continually brought to me for more than forty-eight hours, I will become fatigued. I will have to rest, or I will pass out and be unable to continue my work. It would appear that I am being selfish by getting an hour of sleep, especially if someone dies during that time. However, after some sleep, I am able to continue to perform additional surgery and save more lives. *Without* sleep, I cannot possibly continue to work. One would have to see that I was not being selfish but taking care of a need in me to have the ability to continue helping the wounded.

Consider another situation. If you have ever taken a flight with a commercial airline, you know that as the plane taxis down the runway, the attendant gives safety instructions. After pointing out safety exits and explaining the use of oxygen masks, the attendant says, "Should oxygen be necessary, the mask will fall from a small compartment above your head." The attendant instructs everyone on how to put on the mask, then continues, "If you are traveling with a child or an invalid, be sure to put the mask on yourself FIRST." This does sound selfish, but if you do not follow these instructions and you become incapacitated, you cannot help the child or invalid. You then become a liability, in need of help yourself.

You must give to yourself before you can give to others. Giving to yourself is not selfish; it is being human.

Chapter 22

Role-Playing

*Every time we attempt something new, we play
a role. Role-playing is healthy when it allows
us to be true to ourselves.*

Human beings want to act in a manner that will make
them acceptable to themselves as well as to others. To
help us along, we must do some role-playing with our
actions. Many times people have difficulty with role-playing saying, "If I am role-playing it is not the real me and I
am being a hypocrite." This is simply not true. You will find
role-playing is not the act of changing yourself or your personality. There are two categories to define role-playing:
ego-syntonic and *ego-alien*, also known as *ego-dystonic*.

The term *ego* refers to yourself. *Ego-syntonic* is acting in
a way that is in harmony with yourself or your situation,
both logically and emotionally. *Ego-alien* is acting in a way
that is not to your liking logically or emotionally.

In an ego-syntonic role, you find yourself comfortable

with the situation. In most cases the situation will require very little effort, and you will have a great deal of pleasure in playing the role because, in fact, the role is you.

For example, you enjoy daily walks and have done so for years. Walking is an enjoyable part of your lifestyle. You unexpectedly sustain a leg fracture and have to be in a cast for several weeks. When the cast is removed, you find standing and walking very difficult. You have lost confidence in your leg. Walking normally requires much effort on your part. Your doctor may have to convince you that your leg has healed. She may have to urge you to play the role and walk on the leg as you had done in the past. This experience is ego-syntonic because walking is something you enjoyed, and with role-playing again and again, you will enjoy walking once more.

Unlike having a broken leg, having severe depression or anxiety will make you lose confidence in all aspects of life. You are not comfortable being around people, doing chores you once did, or being involved in social activities. Once the illness is controlled, you will not suddenly look forward to doing things you once enjoyed. You have to get back to your premorbid state, the state you were in before your illness. Getting there takes a great deal of determination. You will have to force yourself to play the role by doing the things you did when you were well. This role-playing is ego-syntonic. Doing it will help you start feeling well.

If you are in an ego-alien situation, you will find it takes a great deal of effort to continue in this situation. Over a prolonged period of time, the situation will worsen. Staying in this ego-alien state will increase your anxiety, and eventually you will either have to discontinue the situation or you will have some severe emotional problems. You are dominated by your unconscious mind and are acting in ways that are ego-alien and not making sense to you.

Reflecting on my own life, I think I was the most bashful guy to graduate from Old Forge High School. My bashful state was ego-alien and causing me anxiety. When in college, my roommate was the most outgoing person I had ever met. He was exactly the person I wanted to be. I did not realize it at the time, but I was doing behavior modification while playing the role of me wanting to be him. Shy as I was, every time we were out, I made it a point to talk to a stranger. Next, I decided to go a step farther and ask a girl to a dance. The rest is history. Forcing myself to talk to strangers was a first and necessary step to my success. I continued talking, went to medical school, and became a psychiatrist.

If I had not enjoyed the changes with my role-playing, I would have continued to behave in a shy manner. However, by conversing with others and enjoying what I was doing, I was able to change and become more outgoing. Getting comfortable with my role-playing was obviously an ego-syntonic state because I felt it was right. If the role did not feel right, I would have gone back to my shyness.

Those of you who are confident drivers will understand

the confidence you feel now is not how you felt the first time you got behind the wheel. You were afraid and had to play the role over and over until being a good driver was spontaneous and not difficult. Playing the role was ego-syntonic.

I suggest that all of the things we like to do and do well started with role-playing. When trying something for the first time, whether as a child or adult, we are role-playing.

An accomplished pianist started her career by role-playing. Somewhere someone sat her down at a piano and placed her hands on the keys. In the beginning she probably had a lot of anxiety. As her hands repeatedly played the notes, her anxiety decreased and she played much better. If this is ego-syntonic to her, she enjoys playing and will continue to improve.

A professional third baseman started his career when someone put him on third base with a glove. If he persevered, even with some anxiety, and if playing was ego-syntonic to him, he improved his position and became anxiety free.

The only way to know if an action is ego-syntonic is to try to do it. If the action gets easier and becomes enjoyable, you will know it is ego-syntonic. If the action is ego-alien, you will get more uncomfortable, become more anxious, and will eventually quit the role-playing.

DO NOT BE AFRAID TO PLAY THE ROLE.

Chapter 23

The Theory of Relativity, Not by Einstein

*Understand that your life is relative and
is always in motion. Wisdom is
taking time to enjoy the moment while
still focusing on your goals.*

Two certain facts about being human are our birth and our death. The remainder of human life is in a relative position. This life is ours to explore and to cultivate. In our lives, we try to achieve certain qualities: making decisions, controlling our actions, accepting criticism, and learning to accept our humanness.

Think of life as an endless ladder. There are better rungs above you and rungs not as good as yours below you. The rung you are on now keeps you in a relative position in life. Striving to be on the rung above you is a sign of desire to grow. It is healthy. Believing you have to be on the rung above you in order to be happy will harm you. If you are not happy where you are now and think that a better car, a larger house, or financial security will get you that happiness, it is simply not true. That kind of thinking is neurotic (not logical). It is only a relative improvement from where you are now. The role of the environment-be it house, spouse, job, or wealth-is to enhance or detract from the basic you.

Understand that our lives are relative and always in motion. Wisdom is the ability to take time to enjoy the moment while still focusing on our goals.

Chapter 24

Understanding Interdependence

We are all interdependent on one another.
Realizing this fact is important for our peace of mind.

This topic is close to my heart because I hear it constantly in my office. People want to do something important
with their lives before they die. The answer I give them is
that the most important aspect of your life is that you were
born a human being. That is as important as you can get. We
are born one day, and we die one day. What we do in the
interval is really up to us. It is important we feel good about
ourselves while playing our roles here on earth. We should
participate in life for ourselves and with the hope of satisfy-
ing others.

We are all interdependent. Residents of a long-term care
center need nurses and caregivers; a welfare worker needs
people who are receiving welfare; a doctor needs clients;
and a police officer and attorney need someone with anti-
social behavior. Each of us needs someone, and there is
room on this earth for all of us.

The concept of status among human beings grows out of society. We can have a great paying job, fancy possessions, and earn a great deal of money, but the bottom line is whatever we have, underneath it all we are still human.

God Created Humans—Man Created Hierarchies

I worked for seven years after college before going to medical school. One of my employers was the borough of Old Forge. It was not a status job. Quite the contrary. I was pitching garbage for $4.50 a day. I am currently a physician. Am I a better person now than I was when I pitched garbage? I make more money and have some fancier toys, but the bottom line is I am still the same guy, a human being. Will my community shut down if I move? Will the universe stop existing when I die? The answer is: absolutely no. Simply put, you come, do your thing to your satisfaction, enjoy yourself, and then someday you will go.

The hierarchy is man made, it is positional, and is usually involved with employment. The employer's *position* is superior to his employee's *position* but the employer as a *person* is not superior to the employee as a *person*. If you are working and your boss is picking on you, do not accept it as a personal criticism. In reality, the *boss's position* is attacking the *employee's position*. If your employer, as a person, dislikes you as a person then that is his opinion and he is entitled to that opinion. Keep in mind though, you are also entitled to your opinion.

Society is structured so that it has room for everyone. We are all human beings with varying personalities, drives, and abilities. It is for us to choose what we wish to try based on what is available. There is no special role to play. The end for mortal humans remains the same regardless of the road taken. Society can offer positive and/or negative status to our roles, but it cannot dictate the role we play.

Again, our goal in life:
Give the maximum effort to be all that we **can** be!

Chapter 25

Criticism

Criticism can hurt. But it helps to understand that it is an expression of another person's opinion, not necessarily a truth about ourselves.

People's Criticism, a Backhanded Compliment

Criticism is the act of finding fault, or a comment of disapproval.

If you do something irritating to someone and they respond negatively to this act, you should be human enough to accept the criticism. However, if you are being unjustly criticized, understand that this is a "backhanded compliment." A backhanded compliment is a compliment that is meant as a criticism but that actually compliments you. You are being "put down" because in the minds of others you appear to be in a superior position to them. The one who criticizes you actually sees you in a power position.

Human beings have feelings of vulnerability and inadequacy and need to feel safe in their environment. A belief that another person is superior to us is psychologically tantamount to having our lives threatened. What people are saying through their criticism is that "I need to get you down to my level so I can be comfortable with you." The implication of making you superior is causing them discomfort. You almost want to thank them for making you more than what you see yourself to be.

When someone criticizes you in any way, shape, or form they are not giving you information about you. What they are doing is revealing information about themselves. If you were to stand in front of fifty individuals who are seeing and hearing you for the first time, and these individuals were asked to critique your attire, intelligence, and personality, each would give a different answer. Yet they all see the same person at the same time. Each person critiques you not on ultimate truths but rather on **their** individual likes and dislikes. People are entitled to their own opinions.

If someone tells you they like your sweater, they are not telling you about the sweater, they are telling you about what they themselves like. Or, they may not like the sweater. Understand that if they do not like the sweater, they are entitled to their opinion, just as you are entitled to yours. Learning not to be sensitive to others' dislikes will help you deal with criticism in everyday life.

Understand that criticism is an expression of a person's

preferences. Never make changes in yourself or your personality in response to others or to please someone else unless it is to first please you. Make these requested changes only if it makes you happy.

If I feel you are the greatest person I ever met, what does this tell you about you? Nothing! I have merely expressed to you what I like. I am just a human being. You are still the same person that existed prior to my comments. Ergo, if I find you are the worst person in existence, what does that tell you about you? Nothing! It is only my opinion as a human being.

If God criticizes you, pay attention and change. If it is anyone else, listen and change only if you agree with him or her.

If someone important to you demands that you change and you are unhappy making that change, you will be making it solely for that person. This is an ego-alien situation. Permitting yourself to continue this unhealthy change will result in emotional breakdown or self destruction.

Chapter 26

Permit

Learn to live and let be.

The secret word in life is PERMIT. I feel this
word permit is essential in our lives.

To *permit* is to *accept*. When you permit, that does not
necessarily mean you like or agree with the situation.
But if the situation cannot be changed, you must accept it as
it is and permit it to happen. You are an adult human being,
not psychotic or retarded, and you are on a par with all
other humans. Permit others to be themselves. Permit yourself to be you. As you become more accepting of yourself,
permitting you to be the real you, you will make it easier to
permit others to be themselves and accept them as they are.

Permit = Accept
You are human, not God. Accept this.
You are equal to other human beings. Permit this.
You may criticize or be criticized. Accept it.

You may have to role-play. Permit it.

You must make the best choices available to you.

Accept this.

You may not like what others say or do.

Permit them to do as they want.

Remember:

1. Keep life simple.

2. Accept yourself and others as human beings.

Chapter 27

Someone Forcing Me

Unless someone threatens you with bodily harm,
no one can force you to do what you do not want to do.

If someone asks you to do something that makes you uncomfortable, do not attempt to comply with this request. You are an equal human being, and no one has the right to force another person to do anything against his or her will. Unless someone is in some way threatening you with physical violence, the responsibility for your behavior rests with you. Do not sacrifice your wants to satisfy others unless this is your desire.

Take any example and exaggerate it to the ridiculous to help you understand the above concept. Here is one example:

If your spouse asks you to go to Courthouse Square at noon, remove your clothing and carry a sign stating your undying love for him, would you do it? Most people would answer no. You cannot be forced to do anything against your will without physical violence as a threat. Here again, you have choices of bad vs. worse. Make the choice best suited to you, and take responsibility for the choice.

Chapter 28

Demands On You From Parents And Others

*Many of the people we know make demands
on us. It is important to understand how those
demands affect our decisions and behaviors.*

In our early growth and development, we perceive our parents as God-like. Parents make demands of us to live life as they see appropriate. They make these demands because we are important to them and they try to guide us in the right directions.

As we grow into adolescence and start to make decisions of our own, we may not always agree with our parents. At this point in our lives, our parents try to encourage us to agree with their thoughts and feelings since they are the adults and feel they know what is best for us.

As we become adults, the difficulty in having our own opinions and feelings is that they may collide with those of our parents or other important people in our lives. This may cause some arguments and guilt. We, like our parents, are human beings and we have equal rights as adults. If we understand this equality, then other people's demands should not frustrate or confuse us. We can use our conscious mind to understand the thinking of other people and combine this understanding with our unconscious or emotional mind to make decisions regarding the demands.

If you act purposely to displease others, shame on you. If you do things because it appears right for you and this displeases others, that is unfortunate for those others.

If I enter an interpersonal relationship with someone who I feel will give me happiness and fulfillment in my life, and if this person is not acceptable to my parents, I do not have to forego the relationship for the sake of my parents or anyone else. This is my decision. If I continue this relationship only because it displeases my parents, I am acting in a neurotic manner. If I truly feel this individual will fulfill my life but my choice is not acceptable to my parents, that indeed is unfortunate for my parents.

Humans are equal, and decisions made by each of us should be our choice, not the choice of the person making the demand. Understanding this concept should make communicating easier.

Chapter 29

Being Taken into an Argument: Your Choice

No one has to be drawn into an argument.

You never have to be taken into an argument unless you want to be taken there. If you witness two individuals engaged in an argument, your best option is not to become involved. Do not intrude on disagreements others are having.

If you are asked for your opinion, both parties must agree to accept you as the authority of the matter. Then, **if you choose to be involved**, you can give your thoughts on the subject. Both parties should accept your reasoning as the answer to the argument and abide by your decision.

Unfortunately, in most cases, an outside opinion will favor one party and will make the other party involved more angry. A two-person argument has become a three-person argument. When two people argue, they are attempting to get each other to agree with their thinking. Each wants the other's approval. This is the dynamic of an argument. If you choose to give your opinion, you most likely will find yourself, unwillingly, the center of the dispute because both parties have said their piece to each other, and your opinion will add a fresh idea into the discussion.

When asked to insert your opinion into an argument, it would be safe to say, "Yes, I have an opinion, but since it will side with one of you and contradict the other, my opinion will not solve your problem."

Unless you want to be involved in the argument, you had best walk away.

Chapter 30

Dynamics of an Argument

Insecurity is at the root of any argument.
When you allow another person to upset you in
an argument, you elevate that person to a
position higher than your own.

If you have ever been in an argument, you know how intense and frustrating it can be when someone will not agree with you. You feel angry enough to strike them so that they will see things your way.

The dynamic behind an argument centers on insecurity. The more heated the argument, the deeper the insecurity. Two people engaged in a heated argument feel insecure with one another. By arguing, each person is attempting to gain the other person's approval in order to feel comfortable with the position they are claiming is correct. Each person is literally begging their opponent to agree with "what is right."

When two people argue, each elevates the other into a

position higher than themselves. While you might be call-ing your opponent "a dumb so-and-so," what you are actu-ally saying is "Dumb as you are, I *need* you to give me your approval that what I am saying is right."

Insecurity is the driving force behind a heated argu-ment. Wanting approval for our thoughts and feelings is universal and quite normal. It is when *need* is present that we have a problem. Needing that approval to get comfort-able with our own ideas and feelings, no matter what the cost, is neurotic (not logical). If you are entitled to your opinion, are they not entitled to theirs? Should they not agree with you, will it make your thoughts or feelings less valid to you?

Chapter 31

Anger

Anger is a vital emotion we all possess.
It is important to express anger
responsibly and allow others to do the same.

Anger is an important emotion, one we all possess. Surely it is one of the feelings we would like to erase, but as human beings we must use our emotions and permit ourselves to get angry at times. We have to control our anger so it does not get us into unwanted situations. We have the power within us to understand the emotions of anger vs. the destruction anger can cause if it is not controlled. We should use our God-given commonsense to control our responses to anger.

Anger may be directed at us from strangers, and even from our own children. Since we are all human, we need to permit others, including our children, to show their emotion of anger as long as it is not physically abusive.

When we need to reprimand our children for bad behavior, we deprive them of privileges they have. At this point the child has a normal response of getting angry with us. We must permit them to be angry. It is an emotion they must show. It is not fair to tell someone "I am taking away your privileges and not letting you do what you want, and I want you to show me love and affection."

Anger is within each and every one of us. We should always show this emotion using commonsense and control.

Chapter 32

Love Does Not Conquer All

*Expressing what you want but making no
demands is the key to a good marriage.*

The theory is that we fall head-over-heels in love, get married, have a family, and live happily ever after. I'm sure most of us can rewrite this theory and make significant adjustments.

When we first meet that "right person," we will surely find some faults with them. While still dating, or even while living together, we find many faults in the person we love, but we are willing to accept them. At this point, we are more accepting because of our feelings of inadequacy. Protesting at this point might cause us to lose the relationship. It is fair to say that a person can want and ask for changes in other people, but it is neurotic (not logical) to demand that someone change for our own needs. After marriage, when the dynamics of the relationship change, we are now more secure in the relationship and may become more demanding. If there is but one incompatibility of major significance, the relationship should not be fostered. It sometimes becomes too difficult to accept the faults, and we then find we absolutely need the changes in our spouse to take place. It becomes the difference between *wanting* and *needing* the alterations in the marriage. If we discuss what we want from one another, and our spouse is unable to fulfill our needs, then we will have to reexamine our desire to stay in the relationship. We should know the importance of not postponing discussions about highly emotionally-charged feelings in an intimate relationship.

A marriage should never be a parent-child relationship, with one person dominant and the other person passive. A meaningful marriage should be an adult-adult relationship, with two individuals able to discuss differences and changes they would want from one another but making no demands of each other. As we are entitled to be the person we want to be, the other person likewise is a human being and is entitled to be the person they choose to be.

For example, if two individuals are compatible in nature, they may very well fall truly in love with each other. They may have been raised with different strong religious beliefs but they will love each other as much as they are capable of loving. However, if the beliefs of the religion demand that upon marriage one or the other must convert, they may find this demand difficult to do. They will find themselves thinking that if the other person loved them enough, they would change for them. Their capacity for love is still there, but the demand against their basic nature will make them unable to change.

Understand that the significant phenomenon about human behavior is that "love cannot conquer all."

Chapter 33

Neurotic Love

Not all love is healthy. This chapter helps you understand unhealthy love.

A *neurotic love situation* is one in which an individual wants their partner to receive the exact same feelings and emotions from their relationship. This is not a fair demand. Each human is unique and will bring their own set of needs and desires into a relationship. Too often in a love situation, each individual will have their own ideas on how the relationship should feel. They will try to impose their feelings on their partner and expect them to reciprocate the exact emotions.

You may want steady attention and want to spend most of your waking hours with the person you love. This person may love you but feel they want to spend some time with friends. This makes you upset knowing she does not share your ideas of spending all of your time together. This is a neurotic situation. At this time you can voice your opinion and ask her to change to suit your feelings. If this is not acceptable to her, then you have to make a choice. You can let yourself dwell on the fact that she will not change and that you are not getting what you want, or you can take her as she is. You will have to know that the good points about this person will outweigh the bad.

It is important for you to be happy in any type of relationship you decide to stay in. You are always entitled to voice your opinion in terms of your likes and dislikes. However, if things cannot be changed and you want to continue on, you must ACCEPT THE WHOLE PACKAGE.

Both partners will have to be content with how they each feel and will have to bring love and compatibility to the relationship. If they do, theirs will grow into a long and happy partnership.

Here is an example. You truly feel love for someone and think you are ready to commit to this person, if only he would do as you ask and have that scar removed. You have given your opinion that he would look more attractive without the scar, but he refuses to have the surgery.

Your choice: ACCEPT THE WHOLE PACKAGE, OR GET OUT OF THE RELATIONSHIP.

Chapter 34

Extramarital Affairs

Affairs usually hurt, but they can occasionally help a marriage.

Most extra marital affairs are very destructive and should not be condoned.

What makes one partner stray and another partner stay? Interestingly, and perhaps surprisingly, it has very little to do with lack of love or desire for one's spouse. In fact, it would be fair to say that an affair reflects a need on the part of the party that strays.

To understand why people have affairs, it is first necessary to understand the idea of "attraction." One person is drawn to another. The attraction can hinge on being placed in close proximity to another person. For an affair to happen, two people have to be in close proximity to one another, then the chemistry ignites.

When two people are placed in this situation, a phenomenon called transference occurs. The love or hate you feel for a partner gets transferred to the other person. If you have a neurotic need for that to go further, you will go ahead with the affair. Doctors and patients, attorneys and clients, bosses and subordinates, or workers and co-workers can experience transference, and this is a normal phenomenon.

These relationships usually start off being rather insignificant. As time passes, a mutual feeling of admiration or respect, along with one party's emotional needs, transfers the "attraction" into a more binding relationship. There is a general feeling of warmth and understanding by one or both. It is a feeling that we can discuss problems with someone who understands us and our problems. In the marriage we discuss problems with someone who is also involved in the problem. Ergo, with our "friend" we have a position of relativity and a positive understanding of our problem. With our spouse, we have a positive relationship but a negative understanding of the problem.

If we have a + + position in one relationship and a + - in another, we will eventually migrate to the + +. This promotes further contact and prompts further intimacy (not necessarily sexual intimacy at this state.) There will be more one-to-one meetings to discuss problems, hoping to get the positive feelings. (The fallacy of this relativity is that if the good listener was involved in the problem solving of the marriage, the good listener would eventually be involved and not remain a good listener.)

With the good feeling there will ultimately come positive unconscious body contact, hand touching, shoulders, gentle "friendly" hugs. This promotes fleeting fantasies of "how nice it would be to have someone so understanding" and this could lead to "flirting" sexual fantasy. At this point, the relationship can still be put on the right course if either one is aware of what is happening. However, if neither is aware, it will progress to feelings of love—no different than any love situation.

This presents another shift of emotion. Since we are taught monogamy, we feel it is alien to love two people-ergo, we need to fall out of love with one to be in love with the other. Now we focus on the negative feeling of the + - relationship and on the positive feeling with the + + relationship. I think the rest of this scenario is history. Once sexual relationship between "friends" proceeds, the commitment to each other becomes increasingly more difficult to abandon.

The solution to this problem is for one or both parties to see what is happening and bring the discussion of transference to open conversation. Then stop promoting the activities that will foster the relationship to the point of no return. This occurs when the emotional mind (non logical) dominates the rational mind (logical). If one finds oneself powerless going down this road, get professional help such as psychotherapy.

I am not promoting the idea of having an affair, but I am

trying to help you understand human behavior. Human beings are not monogamous by nature. They are capable of falling in love with as many people as they permit or get too close to. When an affair looks imminent, it is best to handle the situation early, when the logical mind prevails, by confronting the situation and not promoting it. If we continue to feed the transference, in time the emotional mind will control our actions, and, in most cases, someone in the triangle will be deeply hurt. If we control the situation with our logical mind, we can usually prevent the affair from beginning.

Chapter 35

Wait Until . . .

*We are often told "wait until." We can waste
our whole lives waiting until.*

How many times do we find ourselves wanting to do
something special in our lives but find ourselves saying we should "wait until. . . "?

It starts the minute we begin to understand ourselves:

As a child we must rely on others and "wait until" we
are older to make our own decisions;

When we grow into adolescence, we "wait until" we go
to high school and mature;

We near the end of high school and "wait until" we go
to college and begin to structure our future;

We graduate from college and we will "wait until" we
get a job to think about marriage;

When we become secure in our job, we "wait until" we
get married and start to think about a family;

Our families grow and we "wait until" we can retire to
do all the things we wanted to do in our lives.

Unfortunately, many times we have "waited until" it is too late for us to be in the good health or the financial position to fulfill our dreams. We find our life in its waning years, and only then are we ready to start living. How sad to find in retirement that as we were "waiting until," we already lived our lives.

Life can be like taking a trip across country. You start in Pennsylvania and plan a number of stops on the way to California. When you leave Pennsylvania, you cannot "wait until" you get to Illinois; then you cannot "wait until" you get to Colorado; then you cannot 'wait until" you finally get to California. Sadly, you have missed all of the wonderful sights of your trip by wanting to get to the next location instead of being happy where you were while getting to each stop.

How similar is the journey through life. We find ourselves unable to slow down and enjoy the scenes along the way. Keep an ultimate goal in mind that keeps you headed in the right direction, but enjoy each day as part of your life and learn to relax and enjoy yourself. Hopefully, we will reach our goals, but if we do not, we can experience the enjoyment of having lived each day working toward that end.

Life is a continuum. It starts at birth and ends at death. Do not wish your life away "waiting until." Enjoy where you are at this point of your life, and remember that as you "wait until" life may get better than you expected!

Chapter 36

Death

When is the right time to die?

How many times have we heard "He was too young to die," "He didn't get a chance to accomplish things, he died too soon," "I feel terrible for all of the things he is going to miss."

When is the right time to die? Is there even a right time to die? Is there a right age to die? (seventy, eighty, ninety?) Is there an age when it is too young to die? (Infant, teens, twenties, thirties?) What is a normal lifetime? (fifty years, sixty years, eighty years, ninety years?)

If we know that at birth we have given rise to a human that is mortal, and if there is no guaranteed life expectancy (a lot of averages but no guarantees), then each individual lifespan is from birth to death and there is no time or age requirement.

For mortal human beings, birth starts the clock that will

stop at our ultimate and inevitable death. What we choose to do during the interval is living our life. How we choose to live our life is probably dependent on genetic gifts, personal drive, and availability. But, whatever we accomplish during a lifetime (knowledge, fame, fortune, etc.), the ultimate end is death.

Is this bad? Of course not. If we accept our humanness, we know the ultimate end for us and our loved ones is death. Does this mean we should not strive to achieve? Of course not. Prior to our death, we still have life. Why would we not strive to achieve our maximum in any endeavor so that our life and the lives of our loved ones can be as pleasant as possible.

An example of this theory is the ever popular soap opera. Most of these shows started long before we got interested in them and we certainly know they will be on long after we leave this earth. Does this mean we should not enjoy watching the show while we are alive and well? Certainly not. We can come into the story at any point of time and enjoy the story and all of the characters during the time we are watching the show, and you can rest assured that long after we are gone, the show will continue. When is the best time to tune into the show? No one knows for sure but whenever you do, enjoy the story for as long as you can. When is the best time to stop seeing the show? Anytime, because the show never ends.

Such is the story of your life. It started long before you

got here and will continue long after you are gone. If we understand death is the ultimate goal of life for mortals, then there should be no sorrow in grieving for the deceased, since they have achieved the ultimate goal, but rather grieve for the loss the survivor has sustained. Cry because you miss your loved one, don't cry for your loved one. It doesn't seem fair that because someone gives us so much pleasure during his or her life we hold them responsible for such grief and sadness when they are gone.

Chapter 37

The Road to Toxic Brain: Alcohol and Drug Use

Addictions are common in our society.
There is a definite road to the toxic brain of addiction.

It is important to remember that the mind is made of two parts:

1. The rational part, which uses Aristotelian-like logic and is conscious.

2. The irrational part, which does not run on reason and is not conscious.

Individuals who are under the influence of alcohol and/or drugs have what I call *Toxic Brain*. It does not function normally. The brain is not being rational. People using alcohol and/or drugs are very uncomfortable with the realities of the real world. They feel incapable of changing it and uncomfortable living in it, so they do what they feel is the best solution. They decide to change how they perceive it by using mind-altering devices. Their decision is very dangerous because they are distorting reality and not using the logical brain. They will be unable to think logically in their decision making.

A person who is afraid of traffic and has to cross a New York City street may want to put on blinders to cross the street. The blinders may make them less fearful of crossing the street, but the blinders will surely increase their chances of becoming injured. Using alcohol and/or drugs is the same as putting on the blinders. It alters perception. The times when we have a problem in life are the times when we absolutely need the clearest and most rational mind to give the problem the best attention. Using alcohol or drugs does not give us the clear, rational mind we need to solve our problems.

Knowing if Alcohol Is a Problem

I do not know if I have a definition for alcoholism. I do know there is a problem if the very things you hold important to you become threatened by the use of alcohol, regardless of the quantity consumed. The quantity can range from very little to extreme amounts. In any case, if you feel the need to consume alcohol, you have to know the consequences.

On your lunch break at work, you decide to have one glass of beer. It is detected by your employer, who tells you your job is in jeopardy if this continues. If you continue to have that one beer at lunch and you lose your job, you have a problem with alcohol.

If your spouse is very important to you and cannot tolerate your drinking, regardless of the amount you consume, are you willing to sacrifice losing your spouse? If your answer is yes, you have a problem with alcohol.

As you can see, the quantity is not as significant as the end result. Know the consequences.

Your True Feelings

Many times we get the feeling that people under the influence of alcohol and/or drugs talk about their true feelings. I do not believe this is true.

Human beings use their logical minds to function in a normal life. They show and speak their feelings, which are derived from the logical and emotional brain. Toxic brain causes a malfunction in the logical brain. People under the influence of alcohol and/or drugs are not capable of stating their true feelings. They are expressing what their feelings are when they are toxic.

Having a toxic brain is like a calculator operating on low batteries. It is functional but giving the wrong answers. It is certainly not giving the same answers it would if fresh batteries were installed.

Similarly, a person does not express his true feelings when he is intoxicated or drugged. His thinking is not rational.

Think of the last time you were really angry. You probably vented your frustrations on someone close to you. Did you mean what you said in the fit of temper? Probably not. Anger can shut off your logical brain just as alcohol and/or drugs do.

So next time someone who is very angry or under the influence says hurtful statements remember:

The toxic brain cannot reveal true feelings.

Chapter 38

Smoking

If you can quit smoking, you should.
If you have tried and can't, do not punish yourself.

There is no adult human being, who is not retarded or psychotic, who can dispute the dangers of smoking. Do not try to con yourself into believing it is not a harmful phenomenon.

However, we are aware that smoking is an extremely addicting phenomenon and that not everyone can stop, although they may try. If you are an individual who can stop, of course you should. If you have taken every effort to stop and cannot do it because you enjoy smoking, then smoke and enjoy it. Do not punish yourself. There is no way that you can eliminate all of the possible hazards in life.

If you wish to stop smoking, give yourself the best chance by eliminating self con games.

1) You can't tell yourself you will quit when you lose

the desire to smoke. You must stop smoking long enough to lose the desire. If you don't feed an unconscious drive it will diminish.

If a person goes on a hunger strike to prove a point, he does not lose his appetite first and then stop eating. He will have hunger but will not eat to prove his point. If this continues long enough and then the hunger strike is over, he may need to work at learning to eat again.

2) Don't con yourself by repeating "I don't want to smoke" because if you are a smoker you do want to smoke. You can use a phrase such as "As much as I want to smoke, I'm not going to smoke."

3) Don't wean off smoking, just stop! Know that you will be uncomfortable but also know that if you don't feed the desire it will diminish.

Chapter 39

Mental Disorders

*Mental illness requires appropriate medication
and the care of a trained physician.*

Prior to our awareness of brain chemistry, most if not all mental illnesses were believed to have been caused from the environment-parents, lifestyle, and so on-and from "mental weakness" of the inflicted person. We now feel comfortable knowing that most major illnesses (panic disorder, phobia, obsessive compulsive disorder, major depressive disorder, bipolar affective disorder including manic depressive illness, schizophrenia, eating disorder, and probably more to come) are biochemical disorders of the brain and have a genetic flavoring. In time, most of these conditions will be looked upon as we currently look upon diabetes. Years ago, prior to our understanding of diabetes, when a patient was diagnosed as diabetic, the etiology was believed to be their eating habits (diet).

The best treatment for the mental disorders discussed above is a combination of medication and psychotherapy. If we ask why psychotherapy is necessary if there is a bio-chemical disorder, the answer lies in understanding the illness. Knowledge improves the odds of not aggravating the illness. If you are a diabetic, you have a chemical disorder, but the condition is certainly helped if you follow the advice of a dietitian. If we do not cure the diabetes, we can learn to control it better. If we do not cure the mental disorders, we can control them better by understanding them.

If you have a mental disorder, seek treatment and do not hide it. We are all human beings, and it is no sin to have an illness. The sin would be to not treat the illness. Start with your family physician and discuss your symptoms. Do not hold back. If you have ten symptoms, describe them all to your doctor. If you have fifty symptoms, describe them all. Do not feel the need to hold back. I have had clients who tell me they will not give the family physician all of the symptoms "because he will think I am a neurotic." I say, give him all of the symptoms and if that means you are neurotic, then get treatment for your neurosis. A physician's most important diagnostic tool is history. Give a detailed history. **Talk to your doctor.** A branch of medicine that does not take a history from a client is veterinary medicine. Your family physician is not a veterinarian. **Talk to your doctor.**

There are three rules to follow if you have a mental disorder:
1. Do not sell your house
2. Do not divorce your spouse
3. Do not quit your job

Do not make any big decisions until you are feeling better. I can assure you the house, spouse, or job did not cause the disorder. One or more of these may aggravate it but they are not the cause. Eliminating them will not bring about a cure.

The four P's to getting better:
1. Prayer
2. Pills
3. Patience
4. Push

1) Prayer: This does not need any elaboration.

2) Pills: Your illness is a biochemical disorder of the brain and you must take your medication perfectly.

3) Patience: The meds are slow to start. Sometimes they may take weeks to become effective, and once they do start to work, they will not cause a day by day improvement. You may see a small improvement, and then it may disappear. Improvement will come again. It may last a little longer and then disappear again. So now you are on a roller coaster and, like the roller coaster, if you ride it out it will come to a level, smooth ride.

You also need patience since there is not a set timetable to getting better. Each individual responds differently. If you get a fast result, it is the exception and not the rule. The rule is the long roller coaster undulating improvement.

4) Push: By this, I mean you are to push yourself to attempt to function as if you were not ill. This is extremely difficult because the very thing you need to do to get better is the thing you wish to do least because you feel so bad.

If Wednesday evening is grocery shopping night, then go grocery shopping on Wednesday night (unless you have a 102 degree fever, are bleeding, or are in the hospital). If you are at the grocery store just minutes and have to leave, it is permissible to leave, providing you understand that next Wednesday you will be back. Make every effort to get out of the house daily, weather permitting. Go to a mall, sit on a bench, or go to a local bus stop and take the bus to the end of the line and return. Anything to get out of the house. Why get out? Healthy people rarely know how they feel. Their thoughts are in the environment and away from their body-weather, vacations, food, and so on. People who are not feeling well are totally introspective. They are only aware of their body and its feelings, but because they are not feeling well, these are negative feelings. To try feeling well, you need to get distracted from your negative introspection. Home is a familiar place, and if you stay in the house, even if you are trying to stay busy, you will resort to automatic behavior and will continue to have these negative feelings. *Out of the house* is not familiar and offers distractions-people pass by, a baby cries, a car blows a horn. Each distraction takes us away from our negative, introspective feelings. It is a start to feeling well. I do not know if exercise is as important as medication, but it does help most of these conditions. Push, push, push!

Chapter 40

Being Content

Contentment is possible.

If we want to learn not to argue with others,
we have to learn to be content with ourselves.
Three factors that contribute to our contentment are

Family   Work   Play

We are human beings. Because of this, we will focus
different amounts of energy on each category of family, work, and play. Some of us may spend equal amounts of
time and energy at each, and some may spend much more
time with family than with work or play.

The amount of time you spend with each category is not
relevant, but it is important that you put effort into all three
of them. Family and work are important to our everyday
living, but the play is equally important.

Remember to be selfish and take time for yourself. Be content.

Chapter 41

Accepting Yourself and Others as Human

No one is perfect. We are all human beings.
Life is a lot less difficult if we
learn to accept others and ourselves as human.

We must learn to accept ourselves as living human beings and know that because we are human we will not have perfect lives. Human behavior is not a dot, it is a spectrum. It runs from Saddam Hussein to Mother Theresa and everyone in between. We are all human.

Accepting our humanness will enable us to make rational decisions when we are not comfortable in some situations. Understand there are situations that do not permit us to achieve changes we may try to make.

An example I tell everyone is that you go into a grocery store and pick up a package of meat. It is rare that you will find a package to be the perfect piece of meat with no fat or bone and with a great price. You have to make a decision of whether you want to buy this piece of meat or not. You cannot say to the checkout person that you only want to pay for the meat and not the bone or the fat. You have to buy the whole package. If the good parts of meat outweigh the bad and you can accept the bad with the good then buy the package. When you take this package home you cannot focus on the bone and fat. You do not have to like them, but you do have to accept them. Do your focusing on the good part of the meat.

A relationship can be like the package of meat. There are positive qualities about the person that make you feel good and that you like but there are negative qualities that make you uncomfortable. Remember, you are getting the whole person, you cannot break off the parts you do not like about them. As a human, you are entitled to request a change in the characteristics you do not like about this person. If they do indeed change, then that is a bonus for you. If you cannot accept the negatives in this person and you feel you <u>need</u> them to change, you must get out of the relationship because chances are they will not change. To stay in the relationship will cause you much grief and unhappiness. Similarly, if someone wants a relationship with you, they must accept you as you are. They may request a change, and if you can change and still maintain your identity then do it. If it requires you to change your identity, you must get out of that relationship. You may be able to play a role to satisfy a significant other, but it is a role. Roles that are not ego-syntonic can only be played temporarily. What will happen to the relationship when the real you emerges?

You are human and you should never be stuck with something that makes you unhappy. If you have a better option, take it. If you can get a better piece of meat, buy it; if you find a better person to have a relationship with, make the move; if you find a better job, take it. Focus on the positives. Focusing on the negatives will make you miserable. It is your option.

A Closing Message

I will close with a brief message

Have faith in your background, family, friends, community, and your educational training. All have passed the test of time. Most of all, have faith in yourself and in your ability to be human. Have a goal in life, and choose a road that can lead you there, enjoying the journey through life each day. Above all, experience life as it really is:

A reflection of yourself—Beautiful.

About the Author

Guido D. Boriosi, the son of Italian immigrants, was born January, 1933 and raised in Old Forge, Pennsylvania. The proud son of a coal miner, at the early age of thirteen he knew he would one day be a psychiatrist. This, of course, during a time when few people understood psychiatry.

Working many different jobs throughout his youth, from delivery boy for a bakery to pitching garbage, my dad received an educational scholarship to Lafayette College in Easton, Pennsylvania. There he excelled at his studies. Unfortunately, for reasons beyond his control, medical school would have to wait. Never losing hope that his dream would eventually come true, he accepted a position with the state of Pennsylvania and worked his way to become the Acting Chief of Radiation Protection for the entire state. This earned him a salary only dreamed of by his parents. Seven years went by before an opportunity to go to medical school came knocking on the door. Holding tightly to that childhood dream, my dad jumped at the chance to fulfill what he felt was his true destiny. He quit his more than comfortable position with the state and in 1961 enrolled at Thomas Jefferson Medical School, located in Philadelphia, Pennsylvania. This long delay only made him more determined to be a doctor. In 1969 that dream finally came true, he was not only a doctor, but at long last a psychiatrist.

Dad has been Board Certified by the American Board of Psychiatry and Neurology since 1979 and holds a designation of a Life Member of The American Psychiatric Association. He currently resides in Clarks Summit, Pennsylvania and of course still practices full time in Scranton, Pennsylvania. He has been married for 37 years to my mother, Catherine, and has two wonderful children, Tammy and myself.

The book before you is a culmination of over three decades of my dad's work. It serves as not the end of his legacy, but really the beginning. His common sense and logical approach to daily life does work. It is his desire not only to help some but to help all people that has fueled the writing in these pages.

It is my wish that you, the reader, see my dad for who he really is. Not a board certified physician with a bunch of letters behind his name but that poor child of a coal miner with the simple dream to help people. If you have the opportunity to meet him, you can still see a childlike glimmer of hope in his eye, that this world is the best place to be and that now is the greatest time to live, and that being truly happy really is—so darn easy.

It has been an honor for me to write this small piece about my father and I hope you grow to love him. God knows I do. Enjoy the book.   — Marc S. Boriosi